NICE DAY FOR MURDER

for Stew,
enjoy &
thank you!

NICE DAY FOR MURDER
poems for James Cagney

by Kimmy Beach

Beach
at Red Deer
20 Sept 05

🐦 Turnstone Press

Turnstone Press gratefully acknowledges the assistance of The Canada Council for the Arts, the Manitoba Arts Council, the Government of Canada through the Book Publishing Industry Development Program and the Government of Manitoba through the Department of Culture, Heritage and Tourism, Arts Branch, for our publishing activities.

The Canada Council | Le Conseil des Arts
for the Arts | du Canada

MANITOBA arts COUNCIL
CONSEIL DES DU MANITOBA

Canadä

Cover design: Manuela Dias
Interior design: Sharon Caseburg
Printed and bound in Canada by Friesens for Turnstone Press.

Second printing: April 2004

Canadian Cataloguing in Publication Data

Beach, Kimmy, 1964–
 Nice day for murder

ISBN 0-88801-260-8

 1. Cagney, James, 1899-1986—Poetry. I. Title.
PS8553.E22N52 2001   C811'.6   C2001-910052-3
PR9199.3.B37595N52 2001

for Dawn Andrea Beach
1978-1998

ACKNOWLEDGMENTS

deepest thanks to my husband Stu "The Butcher" Beach.

many thanks to my editor, Dennis Cooley, everyone at Turnstone Press, and Robert "Big Daddy" Kroetsch. thanks to Bert Almon at the University of Alberta, and to T/Ed Dyck and Birk Sproxton at Red Deer College.

thanks to Holly "Sugarlips" Borgerson Calder, Rebecca "Legs" Campbell, Heidi "Pinstripe" Greco and Catherine "The Kid" Greenwood, to Di Brandt, to Lori "the Blonde Alibi" Claerhout, to David H. Elias, to Heather "Charly" Kitteringham, to CBC Latenight for playing *Man of a Thousand Faces* in 1989, and to that guy at the U. of A. who gave me my first Jim Thompson novel.

deepest thanks to *Sage Hill Writing Experience*, to my instructors and fellow *experients* and especially to Steven Ross Smith. thanks to the Monks, Friars and staff at St. Peter's and St. Michael's, especially to Father Demetrius and to the late Friar Lucian Kemble. thanks to Friar Dominic, and to Brothers Paul, Randy, Kurt, Basil, Thomas and Anthony for companionship and joyous chanting.

thanks to my family and friends, especially Griffin "Frog-Legs Mahoney" Cork and Jalesa Briault, the Boss of me.

"I like it best my Jimmy" is for Robert Kroetsch.

"They meet at the Breakfast Table . . ." is for Dave Elias and Dennis Cooley.

the title *Nice Day for Murder* and several of the lines in the title poem are from *Angels with Dirty Faces*, Warner Bros., 1938. some of the lines in "This little boy's beginning to get on my nerves, that's all" and the quote

in "I like it best my Jimmy" are from *The Public Enemy,*
Warner Bros., 1931. lines in italics in "Once a Song and
Dance Man," the cover image, and the epigraph to "the
pretty killer" are from *The Complete Films of James
Cagney* by Homer Dickens, Citadel, 1993. the epigraph
to "Lefty" is from *Cagney by Cagney,* Doubleday, 1976.
some of the lines in "No, and I ain't your 'kid'" are from
Blonde Crazy, Warner Bros., 1931. the phrase, "The
Most Beautiful Ass in Christendom" appears in *Cagney*
by John McCabe, Knopf, 1997. "My poor delicate little
rosebud" is a line from *G-Men,* Warner Bros., 1935.

some of these poems have appeared, in slightly different
form, in *grain, Chickweed: Sage Hill Poetry Series #1*
and *Other Voices.*

TABLE OF CONTENTS

NICE DAY FOR MURDER

Blazon for Jimmy

I'd start
with his hair
I'd be writing for hours about orange
Your orange curls are as orange as
        orange   oranges
I'd have to stop   not imagine it in
my sweating palms   tangled
his tongue
pushing my mouth

I'm thinking of his mouth now but
this stanza (technically) should be
about his eyes.
I can do that.
They were blue (if the movie poster was meant to charm me)
Or brown (if the intent was intimidation and violence).
I prefer to think they're a dark grey like 1930s film stock
The colour so unimportant it's not worth mentioning
Except this is a blazon and one must
mention the eyes of the beloved.

He had a habit of biting
his lower lip
just before he grabbed
the woman by the waist
yanked her
I imagine bodies colliding
and he lifts her chin to his
moist mouth
and I know she can feel

~

I better shut my mouth.
somebody'd think there's only one
thing on this dizzy broad's mind:
That place where his pinstripes meet and fold
The tug of silk the double breast
of his jacket hiding it

Oh Jimmy
Forget this poetic bullshit and
get the christ over here.

my tough

you blaze a hole in my west
wall and
            saunter in
you do it all
the time you and your toughs
packing all kinds of
heat you carry yours trained
lovingly on me

you pull me to you
            slide your cool
gun down my back

you're one swell dish
you say   *baby*
time I checked you out
take my left hand in your mouth and

naturally I tell you
stick your pin
-striped thigh to mine
            and flex

if I run will you shoot me?   I say

try it, doll

I know it's just that old you
-really-got-a-hold-on-me dream
            I don't run
why the hell would I?

found in Jim's desk 1

Mr. James Cagney
c/o Warner Bros. Studios
Hollywood, California

12 May

Dear Mr. Cagney,
    My name is _____,* and I am truly your most
faithful fan in the world. I think other actors like John
Barrymore are good too, but I think you're the best.
There's nobody like you in Hollywood, maybe even the
world.
    Would you please send an autographed picture for our
fan club wall? We have a club called "The Public
Enemys" because we love your movie "The Public
Enemy" a lot. Do you like our name? You could sign the
picture: "To the Public Enemys what a great name for a
fan club James Cagney" or maybe you could just say "All
the best. Love James Cagney" but you don't have to say
"love" if you don't want to because of your wife.
    We have 4 members so far, and everybody in town
knows about you because of the notes I put up on the
street lamps. I drew a pretty good picture of you. Maybe
when you write back if you ask to see it, I'll send it
along.

I wish you all the best of luck with your movies, and you can be sure that I will see every one of them as many times as I can!

Yours always,

*[name excised]

This little boy's beginning to get on my nerves, that's all
[from Mae Clarke who took a
grapefruit in the face from Jimmy
in *The Public Enemy* 1931]

ain't like I was askin for it, mug
you know drinkin before
breakfast ain't good for you and
all's I said was
maybe you found someone you like better

why, you was so sweet when we first met
remember you sat down next to me
at the Black and Tan
          you whispered
stuff I didn't even know was legal
all sorts of stuff bout you and me
havin a wild time over on the west side

but this morning
you shove a grapefruit smack! right in my kisser
grapefruit juice in the eyes, that hurts you mug
now whatcha go and do that for
smudgin up my pretty face?

tomorrow when you show up for breakfast
struttin around here like a prizefighter
in those fancy silk pyjamas
and your eyebrows all knotted up like they get
and your curls all over
I'll be holdin that little gun you gave me
you get me steamed baby and
your face is gonna be drippin

8

P.S. Why stop there, big tough boy?

you got a thing for fruit, Jim

but why stop with the grapefruit, Jimmy?
oh, what fun we coulda had
whipped cream, squishy plums   bananas
those not quite ripe ones
why stop with the grapefruit, lover?

imagine me covered in crushed
raspberries your mouth
pickin them from me
the juice dribblin between my
legs   my breasts
I coulda lived with that
me an over-ripe melon your allover
hands my raspberry thighs

our warm little room coulda smelled of
strawberries and peaches baby
if only you hadn't stopped
if only you hadn't

found in Jim's desk 2

Mr. James Cagney
c/o Warner Bros. Studios
Hollywood, California

31 May

Dear Mr. Cagney,
    Hi, it's me again. I guess now you're so famous in
Hollywood, you don't got much time for fan mail (Ha Ha!)
I was hoping you would send along an autographed
picture by now cause all the members of "The Public
Enemys" are counting on it. We have 7 now, and that's a
lot of fans for one town!
    Listen, Mr. Cagney if you're too busy, that's jake, but
maybe you work with somebody could bring you the
picture and you could sign it, then they could just mail
it to me. I put my address on the bottom of the letter
cause I think you must of lost the last one.
    How's your wife, Billie? I know her name because it
was in Photoplay. She's real pretty. One of my friends
says I look just like her. Maybe I do. Anyways, I went to
the beauty parlor and got my hair dyed blonde like hers
and I even got the finger waves too. I sent you a picture
of me along with this letter. I hope you like it. I posed
like your wife did in the magazine. If you send me one,
too, we'll be even! (Ha Ha!)
    We're looking forward to a letter and a picture, Mr.
Cagney, if you get time. Say hello to Billie from "The
Public Enemys."

Yours always,

Harlow by Moon

a crystal tumbler and three
fingers of scotch   neat
platinum curls in utter disarray

an embroidered ball gown
its shocking split lines
          her thigh

the tumbler empties down her throat
a small wince one drop trickles
and a stumble on
pointed satin heels

one knee bent toward the fireplace
          where she leans three
sheets to the wind

what'd he say before he collected his
lid and blew?

that moon's naked
for you and me doll

          that's a lot of hooey   she breathes
hurls the empty tumbler into
the embers   lands with a floomp
caught by the divan

a moon (barely clothed) peeps
in glinting on shards and a lolling
blonde head

Room 118, Congress Hotel, October 1931

I watch Jean
Harlow over
and over as she pulls
your head to her breast calls you
her bashful boy says she
could love you to death

but you don't live long in this
film you do no more than graze
your lashes across the curve
of her as she tousles you   handles
you   like silk

word comes Nails is
dead and she knows you'd
rather look at a stiff than give her
the tumble she's finally offered and
she lets you go
I'd have killed you first
honey I'd have knocked you
off before I let you go

Baby boy,
I'd have pressed it
nice to your soft skin watched your gorgeous
lashes down the barrel shot you blam in
the right temple
shut my eyes against your blood

after you're dead I'd move the
gun down your
body touch every part of you
with the metal

I could lie with you now your head
on my breast   my head thrown
back till they knock that damn
door in with the butts of their
Tommies   your lashes brush my collar
bone when I breathe, Jimmy
yes, right there   warm and
just above my right breast

your thighs lie
still along the length of mine
your blood glistens on the inner curves of my
breasts and my pistol
dangles from my left index finger four
inches above the hardwood

The Big Brush-off

Parker and Sons
Barristers and Solicitors

15 June

Dear Mrs. _____,

We are sorry to inform you that we will no longer be requiring your services as secretary here at Parker and Sons. Your termination is effective immediately.

Repeated incidents of irrational and disturbing behavior have been brought to our attention, and we feel that we can no longer tolerate your violent outbursts toward the staff. We are also concerned about reports that you have been following one senior partner to his home in the evenings and looking into his windows. This partner has agreed not to involve the authorities if you agree never to contact him again.

We wish you every success in your future endeavours and we sincerely hope that you will obtain professional help for what is clearly a disorder of some kind.

Sincerely,

R.G. Parker, Senior Partner
Parker and Sons

14

none of that Barrymore crap

       he poses naked
wet from the shower
at the big mirror in the dressing room
      What in hell do I need a dressing room for?
      I can dress anywhere.
through the sliding glass of his
Hollywood Movie Star Home
the pool ripples below Billie's breast
-stroke   spiky white cap platinum
finger waves tucked up

Billie doesn't see him Jim doesn't see
what she sees in him   what *any* of them see
in him
      Why me for chrissakes when Dick
      Powell is in the world?
he's not stupid, mind you   knows he's got great
dancer's legs   nice tight ass   big brown
eyes long lashes
clear skin bad guy nose
he knows they love his thick brows
the way his nostrils turn up at
the edges when he's angry and
dangerous   ready
to shoot at the copper's knees

the hair is what does it   rippled
masses of orange and
women want that hair they want to
let it fall let it
curl on their tongues and breasts
      But look at these damned arms. Can't even
      hold them straight anymore.
      Too many years of lifting weights.
too short that's the bottom line

but he won't pull that John Barrymore crap no sir no
boxes for him trenches for co-stars none
of that actor-y Hollywood bullshit

just here to make an honest buck and get his ass
and his wife out of this tinselled hell
out to the little ranch where he can play
farmer   see sky

he takes his generous cock in his thick
freckled hands
   Even this *is freckled*
   Can't escape this bloody red
   -headed body

from the hill opposite (far above
Billie's splash)   she doesn't notice
the freckles on his penis   she is too far
away her binoculars aren't very good
his freckles do not cross her mind

she watches him paw
himself inside a fuzzy black-edged circle

found in Jim's desk 3

Mr. James Cagney
c/o Warner Bros. Studios
Hollywood, California

22 June

Dear James,

   Look. I been telling everybody you're a swell guy, real
jake and all, but I gotta wonder now don't I? What the
hell is going on, Jim? You cheated me with that picture
you finally sent. I mean, all you wrote was "Best, Jim
Cagney." Did I hurt your feelings maybe cause I thought
I asked you to sign something like "love" or "The Public
Enemys." Maybe you're too darn busy at home or driving
around in that new car of yours. I don't remember doing
nothing to you to make you treat me like this. I guess
your house must take a lot of work too. I know it's very
big cause I saw it. I saw you in it. Maybe we could have
a beer together there sometime! (Ha Ha!) That'd be swell!
Cause I got lots of free time now. Lots of it.

   Know what? My favourite part of "The Public Enemy"
is when you say to Jean Harlow "You know all my
friends think that things are different between us than
they are." I like that part because it's you and me
Jimmy. That's us. All my friends think you and me don't
even know each other and that we're not in love. I told
them we're swell pals and we write back and forth all the
time Jimmy. I told them you'd never do nothing to hurt
me, but it's hard to keep my side of the story straight,
what with you not writing oftener to me about how you
feel Jimmy. Do you like the picture I sent? You could see
my shoulders in it, I thought you'd like that.

I sure hope you take the time and write me a letter.
We need to talk, Jimmy, about each other I mean and
lots of other stuff too. You don't have to say "love"
though cause of your wife. I know, you just can't. But
I'm getting pretty tired of waiting around for you to make
up your darn mind!

All my affection,

your ex-boxer's grip
[1927]

you are dreamclutching me always
a hand round my waist
your arm is around my neck
in pretend violence

but your cheek is soft
it's always on me someplace
you're taller than I am
I know you were pretty
short claimed not to
know your own height but
        I know it
I know everything
about you

for me you are taller always
my lips fit nicely into the
curve of your throat
I taste Ben Nye Ivory pancake makeup
you didn't quite get it all
in your rush out the door
to see me Jimmy
me in a drop waist number waiting
on the *Actors Only* steps
and it's the dim New York night
off Broadway

you're not a star yet
hold me Jimmy clutch me
in your night
long ex-boxer's grip

the pretty killer

> It's only with an effort that the pretty killer is decent to
> his dear old mother. . . . It seems to me that Mr. Cagney
> is a rising young talking-picture actor to keep an eye
> on. . . .
>
> *Robert Garland, New York World-Telegram October 1931*

Robert Garland
New York World-Telegram
29 October 1931

Dear Mr. Garland,

I must object to your erroneous remarks of 22
October. Your review of "The Public Enemy" starring the
vile and unwatchable James Cagney was offensive at
every point. My husband and I had the misfortune of
attending the picture during our weekly outing and feel
we must correct you on several glaring errors in your
review.

Not only is Mr. Cagney not "pretty" as you describe
him, he is positively unattractive, and he portays the
gangster figure so convincingly that one must ponder the
possibility of a violent upbringing. I wonder through
what horrors Mr. Cagney's mother must have put the
young lad to transform him into such a hoodlum.
Undoubtedly, Mr. Cagney will never find happiness with
any sort of decent young girl. I am sure he is
surrounded by the lowest and most slatternly stratum of
female Hollywood "society."

To address another issue, I am sensitive, as most
ladies are, to the extreme heat in the cinema houses
these days, and I am sure that my discomfort during the
film was caused by the stifling heat. I believe that the
managers of the theatres strategically raise the
temperature as the film progresses in order to prompt

beverage sales. I wonder if you would confirm or deny this theory in your next column.

To date, I have attended twelve screenings of "The Public Enemy" in an effort to educate other movie-goers as to its vile content and horrifying societal implications.

Thank you for your reviews, Mr. Garland, as they are generally edifying and enlightened. As a reader, though, I do feel it "writ down in my duty," as the Bard would say, to point out when you are in error.

Yours, etc.

Mrs. Frederic Brownlow

Once a Song and Dance Man

i

you would have said:
once a song and dance man
always a song and dance man
and left it at that

it was never that

the delights of violence, the overtones of a semi-
conscious sadism, the tendency toward destruction   1932
and you convincing yourself it didn't
hurt your wife your
children to see the thugs you became just to *put*
groceries on the table as you once
ridiculously announced

hey J.C. how does it slide offscreen?
does it ferment? is it hurled through the air at
wives and children? how is it living
with the Great Cagney? wish I could talk
to your wife

just a guy trying to make a buck
bullshit Jimmy

ii

the Human Wolf they call you with *smiling unreflective*
delight you commit *mayhem and murder*   1961

iii

made your friends turn off the water when not rinsing
their toothbrushes you would go to their houses perch
on the edges of toilets and tubs reach
over turn off the tap while your friends brushed

iv

go home Jimmy
go home to your Bill and the kids
take the praise the
overblown critics the letters from the
smouldering women at
the nine o'clock show staining
the theatre seats with the force of
        their desire

The Most Beautiful Ass in Christendom
[for Joan Blondell]

you can't tap dance like Ruby Keeler
can't keep up to Jimmy's
hoofing   Ruby can't sing a note
but she can dance circles around you
Ruby marries Al
Jolson and
vanishes for forty years

Virginia Mayo's got the hair the sexy
toss of long blonde curls looks
like a million bucks in furs and
spikes   she takes it better than
any of you Jim's hand
over her mouth his forearm
across her throat as
she confesses
that dame never stands up
to him never gives it
back like he deserves   now
she putters in a California
garden painting marigolds

Jean Harlow's eyelids
are lower, sexier   her upper
lip painted higher eye
brows plucked and retouched
with black liner
Jean shows her
breasts when the money's right
poses for Hurrell touching
herself pulls her robe open
for the camera lets
her lids droop   the beauty
spot on her chin marks her

The Bombshell   she is
dead at twenty-six

you are tart, boozy and by 1931
the only dame allowed to slap
Cagney   hard
you do it seven times in *Blonde Crazy*
somebody had to

Jim says you have the most
beautiful ass in all Christendom
he finds reasons to stare at it
on-screen   always checking you
out leering behind you
you never know till you see the rushes

you outlast them all
all the swishing painted beauties
of the thirties and forties   wiggling
your great ass through one B movie
after another finally showing
up as Vi the soda shop waitress
serving up milkshakes and advice
to John Travolta and Olivia Newton-John

you're larger now   older
your ass doesn't hold up the
way it used to corseted into
this polyester apron

John Travolta doesn't care
he kisses your cheek on his way to
the drive-in where Olivia will
leave him stranded   staring
at her ass as she flounces into
the fake fifties darkness

No, and I ain't your "kid"
[a love letter from Joan Blondell 1931]

sure   I could go for you Jimmy
I'd give you a tumble tonight but
it ain't me you want Jimmy
all you love is the dough

these speakies are on us
like a cheap suit
you smirk and lean across candles and hooch
light my Lucky careful
not to catch your sleeve in the flame
careful to brush my breast

Ah nuts   you say
you know I don't
go in for all that mushy stuff.
Just here for laughs, right kid?

anything you say, big boy

I flash ya good
it's nothin like yours Jimmy
not half so big and fancy

I got waiters all over me
but it's too late
by the time you know the gun's at your throat
you gone and spoiled my gin and soda
with all your splashin blood

somethin about you lyin there Jimmy
guts up like that
and your dough tucked who knows where
makes me kinda sorry   kid

Scuse me   Waiter   I'll have another drink
and make it a clean glass, willya?

A Warner Brothers Picture © MCMXXXIII

Night after night the dreammovie casts me as
Virginia Mayo   Mae Clarke   Joan Blondell

Joan becomes me and you lift my face
with your right index
finger under my chin Joan would
stop here   slap you hard   stomp out
I don't   I suck in your machine
gun words   your wet mouth   an orange
curl falls   tickles my lashes

when I replace Virginia or Mae you turn mean
kick chairs from under me smash
fruit in my face you grab my hair and
slam my head against walls Virginia would
go quiet here I
lie teasing and bleed   waiting

to sneak into your most violent
moments feel you brace your spread
legs against the backs of my own
your left hand tears into my arm and I know
that pistol butt is coming
down on my skull

Finally   feel your bullets rip
my breasts
tear open my throat   beneath your sneer
catch a drop of sweat on my cheek

black and white credits crackle

The End
A Warner Brothers Picture

we hold the tableau
the end of the reel
thwacking on the spool

For Father Vlad

[by way of Father Demetrius, St. Peter's Abbey, Muenster, SK]

✸

Jim always said
when a fella needs a hand
you lend the hand first and
ask questions later

when you first meet, Jim takes you
out to dinner always the same
restaurant you have pork chops Jim will have
only sirloin   rare   and a big root
beer float

later, Father Vlad, you receive envelopes
a little cash thirty forty bucks
every so often   a studio insignia you
don't recognize not being a
film buff yourself

good thing too   you need that dough
a Lithuanian monk living in New York
needs a little dough now and again

I suppose, Father, you have to admit
they come in all shapes and sizes
saviours I mean
some impaled on crosses   bleeding
from five wounds
resurrected three days later
another impaled on
the ends of movieknives   bleeding
resurrected Fridays on
CBC Latenight his kindnesses
filtering from a screen in tiny blue
into a sparse and holy room

Lefty

My friend Maud . . . could fight better than anyone
else . . . She was a lefty, and when I boxed with her
. . . she would absolutely stiffen me with that left.

James Cagney

Stiffen him?

[Maud recalls, slurps from a teacup, laughs]

Oh yes, I stiffened him all right, but not the way he tried
to make it sound, let me tell you that. Who did you say
you was?

[a spoon tinkles the edge]

All right, I just don't care for talking to reporters.   Yes,
I know you said that, just double checking's all. Where
was I? Oh yes, Jimmy. That's what I called him, Jimmy.
He says all through that rambling little book how he
hated being called Jimmy. Well that's a bunch of hooey,
if you'll pardon my French and I'll tell you something
else, Miss . . . ? What was it?   Yes, that's right I'll tell
you . . . would you like some tea?   All right then, dear.
You don't mind if I do?

[pours herself bourbon from a teapot]

I'll tell you something else, dear. He liked to be called
Jimmy at . . . you know. How do you say this . . . um,
intimate moments. He'd go take his Almighty Holy
Communion of a Sunday then meet me out back for a
tumble. He liked me saying things to him, you know.
Things. I was supposed to say things like . . . say, you're
not writing any of this down.   Oh yes, I see it now, the

32

little red light. Will this be in a magazine, because I'm very strict about what I say being taken. . . . Yes, I remember you're not, just checking's all. Anyways, as I was sayin, Jimmy liked me to say things. "Oh, Jimmy, gee that's swell" or "I love ya, ya big lug" while he was working away. If you get my meaning.

[bourbon slop in a saucer. loud slurp]

Oh dear, pardon me. Tea. Don't want to waste it.

[a shaky laugh]

Would you like some?   All right. Where was I? Pardon me? Yes, I'm coming to that, fact I was just coming to that just now. Boxed with me. . . .   Yes, I know that's what the book says, I've read the book you know, after all I'm in it. Well, boxing. Back in Hell's Kitchen, there was boxing, sure, but boxing was also what you writers would call a . . . euph-a-mism. You know, when you say something that. . . .   Of course you do. Pardon me. Well, he liked to call me Lefty. Said a gal's left hand did something different somehow that he liked and will you excuse me a second?

[returns to kitchen with the teapot. glug   glug   glug. clink of the lid. steady. steady]

Sure you won't have some, dear?   All right then, I'll just carry on with my story. A girl's left hand could stiffen him better than her right he used to say but may I say he liked both my hands equally I may say. Jimmy had beautiful hands. Did you ever see his hands, dear? Oh I'm sorry, you didn't know him, that's right. He had thick fingers with soft red hair on the back. He was covered in red hair. Thick and soft and his body could melt the heart right out of a gal.   Billie? Oh yes, I knew her, what the hell did you think? She was his wife. Course we was pals, yessir.   Oh no she never knew nothing about Jimmy and me.   Of course, of course. We just had to

[large gulp]

be careful's all.   Well, she wasn't a lefty, you know. Makes all the difference to a boy, that's what my Jimmy used to say, yessir, makes all the difference.

Jimmy, the Lonesome Cowboy,
Joins the Land of the Livin'

Heard tell there's a gal here what's achin' for love
The love only Jimmy can give 'er
That's what I'm here for, that's why I come
To be her Yours Truly forever

Jumped off of this screen here and out of the show
And put on the ol' racing gloves
The pictures'll miss me, sure, that much I know
But a man's gotta have what he loves

My Mustang's awaiting dear, hop in with me
And this ain't no horse I'm atalkin'
You best commence lovin' me sweet, little girl
Or sorry to say you'll be walkin'

Let's burn to the liquor store, lickety split
And let's tie one on, you and me
I hear it's way better, some booze in your blood
To take a girl high as can be

We're stuck to each other now, baby for good
I'm ascared that you might up and leave
That's why I shot you, hon, that's why I snapped
I know you'd not want me to grieve

Jumped off of this screen here and out of the show
Got your body on ice in the cellar
I'm sure that I'll miss ya, yup, that much I know
But the truth is I'm one lovin' feller.

The Autographed 8x10
Glossy of James Cagney
[Big Fork, Montana, 1996]

crumpled into a round frame
plastic rubies in
gelled mounds of Elmer's
the face encased in gold plate
     his nimbus
sports a three hundred dollar price tag

Good Christ
[mental note: swipe three hundred bucks]
at least he touched it
got finger grease on it for sure

aren't many of those around   calls the
Montana antiqueman from behind his
Superman #12
Jim didn't usually sign that way,
see? 'with love'
there in the corner

with love

half the signature is hidden by the frame
its halo of clunky metal
and toy gems leaves the glassless face exposed
it takes on timewrinkle and fingerprint

when you dug it up   I say   *suppose you could*
have found a nicer frame?

made that frame special   he says
I pull my sweater sleeve over
my hand wipe away my unholy marks
the sudden tear on Jimmy's cheek

found in Jim's desk 4

Mr. James Cagney
c/o Warner Bros. Studios
Hollywood, California

03 July

Jimmy,

The people at your work are very mean. I only came cause I need to know why I'm not getting your letters. Maybe I wrote the rong street because I know you been trying to answer. I wanted to give you my real address, but they were very mean and they pushed me Jimmy. How can you let them treat me that way? I know you really love me and you don't want anything bad to happen so tell them when I come, let me in!

I like to watch where you go after you're done on the set. I seen you through the window of the bar with those other stars. I got my husband's binoculars. They're not real good I'm afraid so I can't tell what you're drinking. Maybe if you tell me I could buy you one sometime, just like real pals! (Ha Ha!)

Our fan club ain't so jake anymore. I'm the president so everybody's supposed to respect me but there jealous of our love, Jimmy, and they stopped coming to meetings. They said they wasn't gonna take me being all high and mighty and I couldn't borrow their Photoplays anymore and then they said anyways who did I think I was bossin them around, Miss La-Dee-Da or somebody? Suits me.

I saw "The Crowd Roars" and when you kissed Ann Dvorak, you were thinking of how you would kiss me I bet. Did you like the picture I sent? You can see my legs in it Jimmy but you have to look close. You might have to hide it from your wife because she should just think you love her. At least for now. It's best for everyone.

I love you Jimmy,

my poor delicate little rosebud

Jimmy kneels at my side
I hold him cradle him
his left arm encircles my knees
his right hand low at my hip

a cigarette dangles in my hand
he turns his face and kisses my
nipple through my sequined nineteen
thirty-four party dress
an impulse
not in the script

I dig my hand into his
tangled curls grab a handful
yank his head back
he smells of penny cigars and
bootleg gin

I drop my cigarette to the floor
grind it with the toe of my shoe
Angel   he says
don't get sore
she was nothin
gimme another chance will ya Dollface?

I pull harder snap! he drops
gather him easily in my arms carry
him past cameras cue-card boys
Warner's yellin *hey! come back here*
with my star

we're already
too high to hear him

Nice Day for Murder
[from Leo Gorcey, Dead End Kid
Angels with Dirty Faces 1938]

hey Rocky whattayahear whattayasay?
yer ol pal Bim here
we heard ya was bumped off   toasted   fried
sure sure we knew

but ya don't gotta tell us nothin twice Rocky
we knew the score
we knew you wasn't yella Rocky ol pal
we knew you couldn't of died like they said
Father Jerry coulda bin lyin is what we tink, see?

when you came struttin down our street
the day me 'n' Swing 'n' Soapy tried to roll ya
that weren't nothin personal see
we didn't know who you was
we wanted to touch ya is all check out the
fancy silk duds
see about those muscles is all

after a while we thought maybe you
could come live with us Rocky
be like   well   a Pa to us and not
no sissy stuff neither! just a good Pa
what could learn us a little

40

truth is Rocky, I was glad to see ya burn
you was a no-good mug
I can't count how many times
ya smacked me
cross the head with that wad of dough
I still got bruises up my legs from them
penny loafers you was always
kickin me with
coulda taken em off is all

I don't miss ya not even for a second
ya yella rat

Kiss me goodbye
[from Barbara Payton, whipped with a wet towel
in *Kiss Tomorrow Goodbye*]

I know I started it
sure I threw the knife
but I hardly touched you Jimmy
it was just a little trickle behind your left ear
and besides it was in the script

I watched you walk to the bathroom
could tell you were upset
saw you grab a towel, wet it, touch it
to your face
then turn and look at me

I felt that towel slash me
again and again
my face my breasts my hair
couldn't get my hands up in time

I got the message
you're the star

I love how I got to shoot you
down in that picture
you remember that, Jimmy?
you landed with such a satisfying thunk
it nearly made it all
worthwhile

Make with the Joe

so Jimmy shows up on my
doorstep this morning he's
lookin like a mug and smells
twice as worse

never seen him like that
and I seen all kindsa stuff from my Jimmy

says he needs a cuppa Joe and them
bullets he left here last night
"but Jimmy"   I says
"you told me not to give em over
even if you asked me real nice-like.
you said you was trying to cut down
        on murderin
people you didn't like so good."

"stow it, dame"   he says   which I thought
weren't so sweet.   "hand em over or I'll sock ya one.
say where's that Joe?" he says   "a man's gotta have
his cuppa Joe! move it, doll!"

well officer, you wouldn't unnerstand how
these things happen (on account a yer flat feet)
I put those bullets in the little gun Jimmy bought me
for protection y'unnerstand
and well, it went off, see?

me smilin? what do you mean
smilin? I'm prostrate with grievin
officer honest
I'm sad six ways from Sunday
and then some

Mr. James Cagney

c/o Warner Bros. Studios
Hollywood, California

22 July

Dear Mr. Cagney,

I believe it is in your best interest to refrain from all contact with Mrs. _____. My wife believes that you and she are involved in a romantic relationship and are engaged in sexual activity. She is further convinced that the two of you have acted together in several motion pictures. I found out about all this via the discovery of a letter which I enclose herein.

I am concerned that any violent emotions she may be harbouring toward you or members of your family may place you in some jeopardy. Please take additional precautions when leaving your home and place of work.

Mr. Cagney, you are not the first victim of my wife's misguided ardour, and I am attempting to secure psychological help for her. However, without solid evidence of an attack upon you or your family, it is difficult to take action. I love her, and only want her to be well.

Yours sincerely,

Mr. _____

P.S. Allow me to tell you how thoroughly I enjoyed your fine acting in "The Public Enemy."

44

[enclosed with above]

Mr. James Cagney
c/o Warner Bros. Studios
Hollywood, California

19 July

Darling,

I hate being apart this way. I want to hold you and touch your beautiful hair and feel your lips kissing me on my breasts. I know you feel the same way and it's swell to know. The studio people must of told you you couldn't write to me and they wouldn't let us make any more pictures together. They're afraid of our love, Jimmy cause they know you won't really do it if you're thinking about me and not about acting. Jimmy, just tell them everything's jake. Tell them let me in.

Oh, the way you held me last night Jimmy. I love your big hands, they hold so much of me. I love the rough way you kiss me. I'm blushing Jimmy the things we did. I found my husband's gun. It's a little one. I know what to do so don't worry I won't hurt myself. When I think of those people at the movie place and your wife I get so mad at them for keeping us apart. Pretty soon, we won't be, Jimmy. There's people who want us apart because they know there's never been a love like this in all the world.

When I saw you kiss Loretta Young in "Taxi" I bought some earrings that matched hers in the movie. Did you like the picture I sent Jimmy? She's hard to follow, always getting in the car so fast after filming. Gosh, Jimmy, does everyone live on the same street in Hollywood? They should call that street Movie Star Street! (Ha Ha!)

It won't be long baby,

Jitterbugging at the Black and Tan

in my head it all makes
sense Jimmy and me   I know he could
love me if I was smarter
or prettier if I had a nice
car or prettier shoes or if I wasn't
already married

I need Jean Harlow's eyes to
really get his attention
I need to be in black
and white Jitterbugging at the Black
and Tan all satin slippers
my fur collar higher than my head greased
fingerwaves and white
gloves a hand
at my waist a bow tie at his throat
his top hat tossed to a girl at the door
Toot-Toot-Tootsie don't cry
candles fancy tablecloths he pulls
me closer whispers he loves
me just then somebody
busts in   who would it be?
one of Schemer Burns' boys maybe

hat down low   rain on his
shoulders he pulls his gat and starts
pumping he's aiming for my
Jimmy but I jump
in front of the bullets and I take
them all   all of them wrecking
my ivory gown I'm doing a crazy
bullet blood Jitterbug all my
own and just at the last
minute Jimmy holds me

he knows I'm gonna
die I smile up
at him and close my eyes
my head falls back real pretty
just like in the movies
yeah, I'm in the movies
he'll notice me
now

Prayer to Jimmy #139

[She is sitting 2 rows back watching Jimmy and Barbara Payton in the final moments. It's *Kiss Tomorrow Goodbye*. She's seen it 8 times.]

1 Oh Jimmy, I think you musta somehow crawled inside me and found all my secrets.

2 You can read my mind, I think Jimmy. You show me the way my Jimmy. I'd give anything to put my head on your chest like a pillow. You know everything about me.

3 How do you do that Jimmy?

[She kneels on the floor in front of her seat. Popcorn sticks to her kneecaps. Her clasped hands hit the head of the moviegoer in front of her. MOVIEGOER: *Hey, watch it dame!*]

4 Sometimes I think you're trying to make it hard to follow you and love you Jimmy but I can feel you baby I can feel you touching me. Oh Jimmy, to know you live inside me somewhere.

5 When I die, Jimmy if I go up to heaven I know you'll be there. If I go to hell which I won't but if I did you would be there too because of your love for me.

[MOVIEGOER: *Hey, shaddup willya? Ya dizzy twist.*]

6 Even if I blew and went to live on a boat or something, you'd find me because you'd miss me, miss holding my hand.

7 Sometimes I think I'm scared of the dark Jimmy but when you hold me even the dark is just like daytime.

[On the screen, Barbara aims the pistol at Jimmy.]

8 Jimmy, she ain't got the guts! But I do, I got the guts Jimmy. I'd do whatever you wanted Jimmy. I'd have the guts to shoot you. You like a dame with guts, I know.

9 Cause I'd do anything you said Jimmy anything at all.

[BARBARA {from the screen}: *And you can kiss tomorrow goodbye.*]

10 Oh my God, who does this broad think she is, Jimmy? You'll show her, Jimmy, whip her Jimmy,

where's that towel? You shut her up the first time! Try that!

[MOVIEGOER: *Ah, fer chrissakes lady, willya shut the hell up?*]

11 You know I dream about you every night and when I wake up, sometimes I think it's you. You're still in bed with me. I shouldn't say that but it's true. I'd like to have you in my bed.

12 Can you get rid of all these mugs Jimmy, so's it's just you and me?

13 All's I'm saying is they better stay outta my way, that's all. They better not try and keep us apart. I've heard the way some of these mugs talk about you Jimmy. They don't love you not like I do. They don't.

[Barbara fires. Blam! Blamblam! Jimmy falls. Thud!]

14 I got a bad streak Jimmy a bad streak around these people.

[She climbs up on the platform and touches the screen where Jimmy's head meets the stage. She bangs her fist on the dusty image causing it to ripple Jimmy's face as

if in a fun house mirror. MOVIEGOER: *Hey, shaddup and siddown, ya crazy broad!* From the foot of the screen she fires at the two-storey face of Barbara Payton. The screen tears and Barbara's face is ripped down the centre, her left cheek a black gash. The movie police burst in.]

15 I hate them all Jimmy and I'll just kill them all.

[She turns and fires blindly into the audience. Moviegoers scatter screaming to poorly marked exits.]

16 Hey, shaddup! Tryin to watch the picture here, for chrissakes!

17 They're all out to get me Jimmy. Jimmy keep me safe. Keep me safe. [She drops her pistol and slumps to the stage]

18 Jimmy Jimmy.

[The movie police drag Barbara Payton's stunned and torn face from the seedy apartment where Jimmy lies dead. The Hollywood Police drag her stunned from the theatre where an usher lies wounded. Fade.]

CAGNEY TORMENTOR APPREHENDED!!

by Terry Mahoney, special editorial to *The Star*

Popular picture star and Hollywood gadabout Jimmy Cagney was relieved today to catch word that the unnamed woman who has been tormenting him for months was finally grabbed by the long arm of Hollywood law! Our fine boys in blue caught up with this would-be Bonnie-style gunslinger as she attempted to machine-gun her way into our favorite bad boy's heart. *The Star* is still digging to find out just who this brazen broad might be. Is she an unhappy fan who thinks there's not enough lovemaking in Jimmy's films? Is she a former co-star who was grieved working with Jimmy? Our snitches say that our boy Jim is one of the best eggs on the Warner lot. Everybody loves Jimmy!

The victim of this dizzy dame's rampage is none other than Johnny "The Keys" Batista, head usher and our inside boy at the Marquis Theatre where the doll was apprehended. Seems our loony lass tore the place up. They say they have to get a new screen. Johnny told this reporter (from the torture of his hospital bed where he is suffering from agonizing skin lacerations to his left calf), that the dame in question had been there before. In fact, Johnny reports, he's had to have her forcibly removed from the premises on more than one occasion. What this reporter wants to know is, why didn't our boy Johnny call the flatfoots a long time ago and have them set this dame square? I ask you, dear readers, how does a skirt like this get past the eye of the biggest picture house in Tinseltown?

Mr. Cagney couldn't be reached for comment by press time. Seems he's blown. Skipped town for parts unknown. This reporter can hardly blame him. But I ask you dear readers, would you leave your dish of a wife at home while you went off to hide from a dame? We're not saying Jimmy's done wrong, no sirree, all we're saying is, take the little lady with ya, Jimmy!

Well, here's hoping this story turns out like one of Jimmy's funny pictures. Everybody happy in the end and the bad guys (and dames) in the stir where they belong. This reporter is watching his back on the way home from work today. Any more of you dizzy twists on the lam out there? Count me out!!

not posted

November 2nd

Jimmy,

       Hey Jimmy listen to me. I did it. They're gone.
Bet you knew it was me didn't you? I thought you
might since I sent the
picture of me with the gun. How about that one? Did
you like that picture? Did you?
       Jimmy?
I thought I looked pretty
in it. I'm fuzzy right now
Jimmy. That's how I wanted
you to think of me Jimmy pretty. I left Billie
so she could think about how she's
keeping us apart, but the rest of them

bumped them off all of them.
       You'll probably never get this letter, and if
you miss me bad and try to write me, I
probably won't get it either. I don't think
they let you get mail in here. They made me
take drugs. I'll
bust out soon's I can. We'll be together again
I know we will Jimmy. Jimmy?

I love you I want you touching me

Strawberry Bullets

I stand in the hallway
hands full of unwashed strawberries
bought them special
I know I wasn't supposed to
leave the house but
I know how you love them

your right hand flashes under my chin
the barrel of your revolver snaps
my jaw strawberries bullet from my
fingers splat onto walls floors
your thigh I reel
into a corner   smiling thru smashed lips

you've left your hand sweat
on my ripped skin
I stick my tongue out and lick
the salt it
tastes good sharp
like metal

hey   tough guy
that all you got?

Jimmy talks back
[a love letter]

Right, broad, let's have this out.
The name's Jim, not Jimmy.
I always hated that and you know it.

All that tough stuff, that was just work.
If I were a dentist, why, nobody would think
I go home at night, and say to the wife "hey broad
get yourself in this chair while I put you under and
drill your teeth and where are the kids I
wanna do theirs too."

Play one tough and that's it
you're labelled
fifteen years after you been put
in the ground. I'm Tom Powers I'm Cody Jarrett
No, I'm Rocky Sullivan   Hell I been
called a mug so many times I'm starting to turn
into one and it's broads like you keeping me there.

Let me tell you something, sweetheart.
I never got the last word with any of those dames.
Joan smacked me so hard across the kisser one time
she broke a blood vessel couldn't film for days
and Mae, sure I had to be hard on her with
grapefruits and dragging her around by the hair
but I never wanted that and besides,
they were the ones left alive
at the end of the picture,
when the lights came on
people standing up blinking in the
cone of blue smoke,
never me it was
never me left alive.

just be with me Jimmy

Jimmy
     I'm not quite
myself just now the drugs
got me woozy Jimmy I know you're
there Jimmy

I'd let you do anything
     to me Jimmy
  hurt me however ya
want just be with me
          Jimmy
     that's all
     that's not so much to ask is it?
   Jimmy? Jimmy?

shh   here's a nurse
she's got a needle they won't let
me out to   *ouch!*   see you they
said I'm   *bitch*   dangerous to myself
and others
        I have to close my
           eyes now   I know you're
   there Jimmy answer me answer me
        I love you Jimmy answer me!

Jim makes a call on a Sunday afternoon

Hello, Yards 3771 please.

Hello Pat? Yeah, it's me Jim.　　　Good good. And you?
Good. Listen Pat. That sick twist that's been following
me? Got herself locked up.　　　　　No, locked up.
　　　　Yeah. After she tried to knock off Johnny over at
the Marquis.　　　　You didn't? Didn't you read about it?
Yeah yeah, he's going to be okay, but. . . .　　　No, she's
not under arrest or anything. Not yet. So listen, she
could get out easy. Real shame. Jesus, Pat.　　　Yes, I
know, I'm thinking am I next?

　　　　　Ah Christ, I don't know. The doctors won't tell me
anything.　　　　Well, yeah! Jesus! They should warn a
fella about shit like this when he moves here.
Yeah.　　　　No, they've already done all that. She's
done the psychiatric evaluation and everything and they
say she isn't fit to stand trial so that's it, she's locked up
in the nut house, no charges, no questions asked.　　　I
know! I mean obviously she's trying to. . . . Hang on a
sec willya, Pat?　　　*Okay, honey! Have a good time!*
Sorry. Lunch with the girls. Good thing, I'd rather she
didn't hear this conversation anyway.　　　　Right, right.
What's the world coming to, Pat? I mean, this skirt's
gonna hurt me if I let her. Thing is, I'm afraid she's
gonna do something stupid and she ends up hurtin my
Bill if I don't watch out.　　　　Yeah, yeah, I know. Say,
why is it always the nuts with me? Why don't Cary and
Humphrey get the nuts for a change? How come *you*
never get a nut? Oh, yeah, I forgot. You ain't good
looking enough!　　　　Right! Who'd want that sorry
mug? Ha!

54

Well, I've thought about that Pat, and I
decided I better drop out of sight for a while.
Yeah, but what if she follows me is what I'm thinking,
you know, so she won't threaten Billie.   Yeah,
I've seen pictures of her. I got some, sure.   Well, why the
christ not, she sends me goddamn pictures all the
goddamn time. She's a swell dish, a real looker, I'll tell
you that. But wait till you hear this. She thinks we do it.
 What do ya mean, what's "it"? It! We done it, she says.
We've had sex for chrissakes!   Oh, I think
I'd remember that, my friend. She thinks we do it every
night for hours, we're a couple of dogs in heat.
Now you get your mind out of the gutter, Pat! Ha ha!

              Listen, I know you don't, but this
is how it's gotta be. I'll tell *you* but I don't want you
telling my Bill where I am. I'm going to go be a monk for
a few days.   Sure, I know a place.   Ha!
You're right. I don't think she's getting it regular from
her old man.   Beats me. You said it, pal, my
mug's nothing to write home about.   Okay, but listen,
keep an eye on my Bill for me, willya pal?   Yeah,
Bill's a tough broad, but this dame's got a gun and she's
gone bananas. I got extra guards on but I want her to
know she can give you or Eloise a ring if she gets
scared, okay pal?

          Yeah.   Right.   No, I will, couple of days.
Promise.   Yes, I will. Tuesday.   Thanks, old friend.

Reclining

It's all closing in
on me here. I am made of
stone my hands are made of stone
and my face.

I'm Jean Harlow reclining.
Everybody does everything
for me. I don't even have to
feed myself. All I gotta do is take
these pills and I get whatever I
want. I can call for the
script and my makeup man anytime
I like. I make a big fuss if I don't
get what I want right away. That's
what Jean would do.

~

I found a feather in the
courtyard yesterday.
I asked the doctors here to
run some tests on it. I told them
it must be an angel feather since
it doesn't smell like a human
feather. But even though they
say they're doctors they won't
even look.

To: Friar Dominic
From: Friar Lucian
Re: Our new guest

Dominic,

I want to make you aware of a distinguished visitor to the retreat. His name is Mr. James Cagney. You may have heard of him. He is a motion picture star by trade.

Mr. Cagney is here on retreat, and quite frankly, he fears for his life. I am sorry to tell you that there is a woman who is somewhat deluded regarding their relationship. Mr. Cagney has confided in me to a great extent and I feel honoured that he has chosen me as confessor. I should point out here that our new guest has not attended church in some time and is excited by the opportunity to worship freely.

Under the circumstances, I feel that secrecy is the best defence. Although the woman in question is under psychiatric observation at present, please be wary of a woman with blonde or red "finger wave" curls. She may claim to be Mr. Cagney's wife or lover. In fact, Mr. Cagney's wife has no knowledge of his whereabouts, and I am convinced that he has not taken a lover. I know that our policy is to refuse no one sanctuary, but in the interest of our guest's safety, I suggest that, with God's help, we keep our eyes open.

Thank you for your attention to this matter,

Luke

Cinderblock Littleness

I smell the heat kissing your
shirt to your back I can
smell you   lie on my belly naked
my tongue tasting
the crack below
the door where you pass blue
and sticky smell of
cigarettes and gin

silent for your
wiry curls though I know
you're just down the hallway
down the thin hallway

in your
own room you hum
Cohan in a raspy baritone
She's my Yankee Doodle Joy

I crawl hunted into crisp
sheets picture
your voice your throat in
this cloistered cinderblock
littleness it won't
burn I tell myself I
shouldn't try

I think you could resist me

I know you won't

Slipped under the door,
Room 15, St. Michael's Retreat

Hi Jimmy,

I found you baby. It's me, _____. I'm just down the hall in room 13. I'm here right now. Please don't bother the Friars about me. I have the little gun I told you about and I know how to use it. The Friars won't believe anything you say anyways. If you try and tell them about me, I'll just kill them all and I'll kill you too. I know the Friars don't have any guns. I changed the way I look, and I told them I'm going through a divorce and I need a break from all the stress. I am, you know. Getting a divorce I mean. My husband found out about us Jimmy and he said if you loved me so goddam much, you could have me. Suits me I said.

Someday I'll tell you all about how I got out of that awful place but none of that matters right now. All that matters is you and me can be together Jimmy. No mean people, no Billie, no nobody.

Why don't you come to my room. There's only one thing I need from you Jimmy and I think you know what that is. We need to be together tonight Jimmy. If we're not, I'll just kill everyone and I won't even care. I want to play a movie scene with you Jimmy not just a kissing scene a real love scene.

Bring your big soft hands to me Jimmy and your long long lashes. I can touch you how Billie is ashamed to. I can put your cock in my mouth and let you move your hips so it feels good for you. Billie won't do that I bet. I'm not ashamed to touch every part of you Jimmy.

Get over here Jimmy right now. I know you're in there I heard you moving around. I'm waiting. Come out of your room, turn left, go past the first door and then next one on the right, knock. That's 13, and that's where I am right now waiting for you. In about two seconds I better hear your doorknob click and I better hear you coming down that hallway ready for love.

I like it best my Jimmy

when you let me tie you to the
posts with these thin ribbons
from my sewing basket   brought em special
thinkin gee,
we might need these ribbons
Jimmy and me
a ribbon at each of your wrists your
arms spread to the rusty old posts
one thin band around your
ankles tied to this spring
under the mattress

come here baby   you say   *come here*
in a minute Jimmy   I'm just gonna
stand over here and look at you
Jimmy you look thirsty
I can put a little wine on your lips
I can say Jean's lines Jimmy   I'll say,
"Oh, Jimmy I could love you to death" then
what do you say Jimmy?
I say shaddup and get your can over here

in a minute Jimmy
you know you look like mine lyin there
naked and mine gorgeous arms
and thighs and Jimmy how can I talk
about what we do together how I
use my body to smother your sneer
your growls muffled me wailing
wakin up friars you whisperin
shh baby shh
do I gotta sock ya one?

Jimmy are your
hands okay? how bout your feet?
Jesus dame stop talkin and hop on board
we're in for a swell ride you and me

like he'll ever eat again

my baby lies down for me pours it
all over me likes to bite me make me feel
it chews on me like he'll never eat again

Jimmy's Confession

I been tryin geez how I'm tryin
it's been a week since
I been coming to her and I come
every goddam night
this dish really gives me the goods
no two ways about that

and oh I love it I love what she
does to me   I let her
tie me up been lettin
her bleed me beat me take me
hard suppose I could bust these
ribbons   I don't

          some tough guy
          tied to a twist's bed and likin it

Christ Jim, what the hell's happened to you?
I gotta break it off   I gotta tell her I'm gonna blow
I'm goin screwy in here
she'll turn me into a stiff if I don't
take a powder and fast

tomorrrow   maybe
she says she has something special
planned for tonight   geez my
wrists are sore   god help me

They meet at the Breakfast Table
St. Michael's Retreat
Lumsden, Saskatchewan

(retreatants' dining room   rectangular tables napkin
holders   wallsize mural of St. Francis and his pals
eating melons eggplant from a big tray   Jimmy sits
down at my table   I look up   see him
dressed 1931   32 years old   takes off his hat
smooths his orange curls   )

Hiya doll. Thanks for last night.

Jimmy
I kinda figured you'd show up here this morning.

(cutlery and conversation scrape   on plates)

What are you still doin in this place, baby?
Ain't we had all the fun we're gonna?

I gotta finish you Jimmy, finish writing you down
off that big silver screen.

You had to write
about me or nobody. I wouldn't have it
no other way, see?

I been handcuffed to you for years you know that Jimmy
strapped to your thigh like a cheap holster
the kind you always wore in the movies
could you feel me Jimmy?

Sure, doll. I felt you. You feel me?
That was Jimmy standing behind you when you
wrote those sweet
lines for me. Remember how you
used to tingle when you ran your hand behind your neck?
That was your Jimmy. Oh, we was great together baby.

Say, doll, what's wrong with you, why
that funny look in your eyes?

What do you want Jimmy?

Come to ask you a favour dollface. Now I been
nice and we've had plenty of laughs together, baby, but
ya gotta leave me alone, let me
R.I.P. as they say. Ya gotta get out
of my head. It's killing me
baby, what do you want from me?

Tit for tat, Jimmy. I'm gonna
kiss you now Jimmy. Gonna lay
one on you. Member when
you used to lean over those
broads in the pictures? God
I loved to watch you do that, Jimmy.
You wanna know what I want
from you this morning Jimmy? Here's
what I want from you.

(lift him by his tie   take the back of his head in one
hand   grab his ass with the other   plant the
greatest kiss he ever had on his lips)

Is that what you wanted? Okay, how bout you and
me starting over again, real nice like.

I got somethin else in mind Jimmy.

(see half grapefruit on the next table   think about it
go for the pistol instead   point it at him)

What about all those times you
weren't there for me, Jimmy?
What about that? Huh, Jimmy?
All those letters you never
answered, all the times I tried to get you
to love me. I knew you loved
me Jimmy, you just didn't show it
so good, that's all. I'm a
good looking dish, ain't I Jimmy? Ain't I?
I thought you felt something for me
last night Jimmy, but now I ain't so sure.

Say, you're looking a little pale, Jimmy. I never seen
that look in the movies. You know Jimmy, I'm glad
we both showed up here. I love you Jimmy but I
gotta bump you off. Once and for all, baby.
Just like in the movies, Jimmy only this time
you ain't comin back see? The
big sleep, Jimmy, the curtain call.

Wasn't it always you and me
in the movies baby? Wasn't it always you
and me? Wasn't it baby? Baby, I was just
sayin my lines. It was
in the script for chrissakes!

Aw, don't look at me that way Jimmy I gotta do it, I tell
ya, I gotta do it.

(level the pistol   aim at his forehead   "no please
baby" comin' outta him   pull trigger   see bullet
enter head   few stray hairs suck into the wound
keep pistol still case he ain't dead   he slumps
hands dangle between his legs under the table   blood
pools between napkins   back of his head gone fired
across the room   it hits the mural with a thud
slides to the floor in a raspberry pulp   nobody
notices   Friar Dominic starts wipin tables   one
last kiss for the gorgeous redhead   wipe his blood off
my mouth with the back of my hand   smooth my
orange curls   put his hat on and beat it

fade to black and white   )

So long, suckers

well, what the hell you still sittin out there for, ya
mugs? show's over. I gotta blow. don't let the door hit
you in the ass on the way out, and remember what
Rocky Sullivan learned ya, *don't be a sucker*

James Cagney was born in "Hell's Kitchen", New York City in 1899 to Irish immigrants Carolyn and Jim Cagney. Before turning to acting, James tried his hand at boxing, street fighting (where he kicked some serious ass), and baseball. In the late teens and early '20s, he gained experience in the Grand Street Follies where he met Joan Blondell, a former Ziegfeld Follies girl who would become a life-long friend. Jim moved to Hollywood with his wife Frances ("Bill") in 1930 and played bit parts for Warner Brothers Pictures until his star-making role as hoodlum Tom Powers in 1931's *The Public Enemy*. He was a star by his fifth film.

Cagney won his only Best Actor Academy Award in 1942 for his portrayal of Vaudeville great George M. Cohan in *Yankee Doodle Dandy*. Jim always wanted to be remembered as a "hoofer," a song-and-dance man, and he made a few musicals (most forgotten with the exception of *Yankee Doodle Dandy*). But it was his tough guy pictures of the 1930s and '40s that paid the bills.

A good cross-section of Cagney films, if you find you're interested, is (in this order): *The Public Enemy*, *Angels with Dirty Faces*, *The Roaring Twenties*, *Each Dawn I Die*, *Yankee Doodle Dandy*, *White Heat*, *Love Me or Love Me*, *Man of a Thousand Faces* (in which he plays the great silent film star, Lon Chaney), and *Ragtime*, Cagney's last feature film. I suggest lots of wise-ass friends and greasy popcorn while watching these pictures.

James Cagney died cracking a joke at the breakfast table one morning in 1986: a result of complications from diabetes.

I never met him.